AIR FRYER
Ultimate Cookbook

Kelly Cohen

The Quick & Easy Guide to Delicious Air Fryer Meals

Air Fryer Recipes – The Complete Air Fryer Guide

Curated Easy Air fryer Recipes for your Favorite Meals!

Kelly Cohen

Thank you for joining me in the kitchen!

I hope these curated timeless recipes will entice you to cook more meals at home and ease the burden of meal planning!

What you will find:

The table of contents is broken down into five main categories with sub categories.

A bit of a bonus.

There's always been a struggle between healthy conscious eating and flavor profiles. I've grown up in Texas with my Grammy's buttermilk fried chicken. To this day it is still one of my favorite dinners, but I always feel slightly guilty after eating it so I've started to eat my fried meals with fruit infused water.

In this recipe cookbook I've included some of my favorite fruit infused waters that would pair great with these delicious Air fried meals!

Cheers,
Kelly

The Art of Air Frying

What is Air Frying?

It's a wonderful alternative to deep frying your favorite proteins and vegetables. Instead of using a bucket full of hot sizzling oil, an Air Fryer cooks by circulating hot air around the food at a very high speed.

Air Frying produces a delicious crispy layer around the foods with very minimum oil, and it does not compromise the taste or texture of the food. By using relatively less oil to "fry" proteins and vegetables, it has become a very popular alternative to traditionally deep fried foods, which can increase the risk of obesity and cardiovascular diseases.

What can you Air Fry?

Air Fryers have become a staple appliance in many households. The Air Fryers in the market comes with adjustable temperatures and timers for very precise cooking, and you could Air Fry just about anything. It works great with chicken, beef, pork, seafood, and many of your favorite vegetables. In this recipe cookbook you will find a variety of Air Frying meals that would suit your entire family.

This recipe cookbook was designed with the **Philip's Air fryer** and the recipes are designed for 2-6 servings, because we found that to get the best tasting results is to avoid overcrowding the cooking basket.

Table of Contents

Introduction

Welcome to the Air fryer Cookbook Edition. We are very excited to share with you some of our curated favorite Air fryer recipes! The Air fryer of our choice is the **Philips Airfryer**, we love the sleek design and it blends in great with any kitchen decor.

Our recipes are designed anywhere between 2-6 servings. The reason behind smaller serving sizes is because we wanted to achieve the best results when cooking with the Air Fryer. We found that to get an even crispness in all our meats, seafood, and vegetables it is best not to crowd the cooking basket. For the best results it's recommended that the ingredients be cooked in layers or small batches.

In here, you will find your favorite easy to prepare and easy to cook Air fryer recipes for chicken, beef, pork and all kinds of seafood and vegetables. These recipes make great dinner entrees or delicious appetizers for the whole family to snack on.

This recipe collection are also very versatile and would make great lunches, weekend dinners and even holiday feasts that will surely impress your relatives and in-laws!

We sincerely hope you enjoy this Easy Air fryer Cookbook as much as we did cooking our way through all these great recipes.

Disclaimer: Cook times and Prep times are suggested times based on trial and preferences. The cook times are also recommendations from the Philips Airfryer manuals that have been adjusted by our team. We have provided "Notes" sections in the recipes for you to add in your own personal tips and tricks on how to make *your* perfect dinner entrée.

Philips Airfryer

How to Use your Philips Airfryer

- Before cooking, allow sufficient time for the Air fryer to reach the desired temperate (approx. 3 minutes).
- Before cooking, spray or brush the cooking basket with olive oil, this will help prevent food from sticking to the cooking basket.
- Do not overcrowd the cooking basket, the Philips Airfryer is designed for smaller servings 2-6 servings is recommended. If you would like to increase serving size, then it is best to cook the food in batches.
- At the end of every cooking cycle, empty the oil/grease in the bottom tray.

How to Clean and Care for your Philips Airfryer

- After every use, it is recommended to use a moist towel to wipe the outside surface of the air fryer.
- To clean the cooking basket, soak it in hot soapy water to loosen food debris, and then you can scrub with a non-abrasive sponge or brush, or follow the instructions for dishwasher best practices. After the cooking basket is cleaned, it's recommended to sprints a bit of lemon water over the basket. This will help reduce the greasy cooked food smell in your Philips Airfryer.
- To clean the heating element, use a soft damp cloth to wipe away debris/oils, make sure your Philips Airfryer is completely cooled and off before you proceed. DO NOT use anything abrasive to clean the heating element.

Chicken Cuts

Parts

1 - Breast
2 - Drumstic / Leg
3 - Thig

4 - Wing
5 - Back
6 - Neck

Parts

1 - Breast
2 - Drumstic / Leg
3 - Thig

4 - Wing
5 - Back
6 - Neck

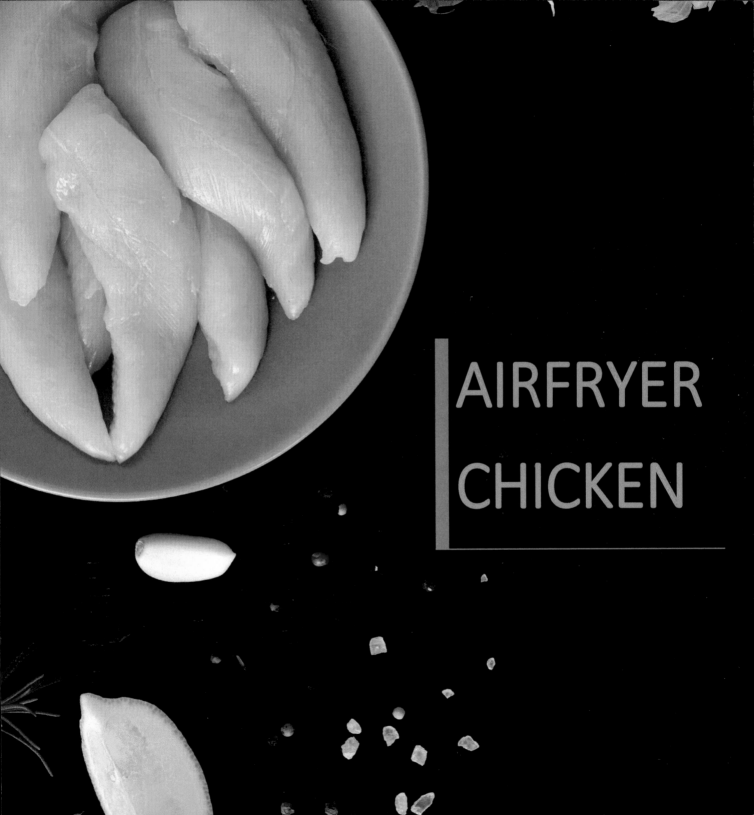

AIRFRYER
CHICKEN

Chicken Tender Strips

COOK TIME
15 MIN
PREP TIME
10 MIN
SERVINGS
4 SERVINGS

INGREDIENTS

- 3 pound chicken tenders cut into strips (this should give you 4-6 strips of chicken)
- 1 tablespoon salt
- 2 tablespoon pepper
- 1 tablespoon soy sauce
- 1 tablespoon sesame oil
- 1 cup breadcrumbs
- 2 cups panko (Japanese Style breadcrumbs)
- ½ cup flour
- 2eggs

PREPARATION

1. Season chicken strips with the following and set aside:
   - 1 tablespoon salt
   - 2 tablespoon pepper
   - 1 tablespoon soy sauce
   - 1 tablespoon sesame oil

2. Toss breadcrumbs and panko with flour, set aside.

3. Beat the eggs and coat your chicken with it, then dip into panko breadcrumb mixture until well coated.

4. Preheat Air Fryer to 350 F then lay the strips evenly in cooking basket and cook for 15 minutes. Set timer. Once timer goes off, cook for another 5 minutes at 390 F.

5. Serve with your favorite dipping sauce and a sprinkle of fresh pepper and a cucumber salad.

Deep Fried Buttermilk Drumsticks

COOK TIME
25 MIN
PREP TIME
15 MIN
SERVINGS
4 SERVINGS

*Please note this recipe is for 4 servings (2 drumsticks for each person) to get a more even and golden brown surface it is best to cook it in batches rather trying to stuff it all into the cooking basket (unless you are using small sized drumsticks)

INGREDIENTS

- 8 medium sized drumsticks
- 2 tablespoon dried parsley flakes
- 1 tablespoon salt
- 4 tablespoon pepper
- 4 tablespoon soy sauce

- 2 tablespoon sesame oil
- 2 cup breadcrumbs
- 1 cup flour
- 2 cup buttermilk

PREPARATION

1. In mixing bowl whisk together the following ingredients:
- 2 cup buttermilk
- 2 tablespoon dried parsley flakes
- 1 tablespoon salt
- 4 tablespoon pepper
- 4 tablespoon soy sauce
- 2 tablespoon sesame oil

2. Add drumsticks to the buttermilk mixture and coat evenly, let marinate for 5 minutes.

3. In another bowl mix together the breadcrumbs and flour and gently season with some salt. Set aside. Preheat Air Fryer to 350 F, once it's reached desired temperature dip the first 4 drumsticks into breadcrumb mixture and lay it out evenly onto cooking basket and cook for 15 minutes, set timer. Once timer goes off, cook for another 10 minutes at 390 F.

4. Repeat process for the next batch. Serve with your favorite pasta or salad on the side.

Hot and Sweet Chicken Breast

COOK TIME
20 MIN
PREP TIME
10 MIN
SERVINGS
2 SERVINGS

INGREDIENTS

- 2 medium size chicken breasts
- 1 tablespoon salt
- 2 tablespoon pepper
- 2 tablespoon chili flakes

- 2 tablespoon chili oil
- ½ cup packed brown sugar (divided for each breast)
- 1 tablespoon sesame oil

PREPARATION

1. Season the two chicken breast with the salt, pepper, chili flakes, chili oil and sesame oil in a bowl. Make sure the breasts are well coated.

2. Preheat Air Fryer to 375 F then lay the breasts evenly in cooking basket and sprinkle the brown sugar evenly over each chicken breasts. Cook for 20 minutes. Set timer.

3. Serve with brown rice and a side of your favorite veggies and a crack of fresh pepper.

Notes

_____
_____
_____
_____
_____
_____
_____
_____
_____
_____

Popcorn Chicken

COOK TIME
20-25 MIN
PREP TIME
10 MIN
SERVINGS
2-4 SERVINGS

INGREDIENTS

- 4 pound chicken tenders cut into small nugget size roughly 3cm in diameter
- 1 tablespoon salt
- 3 tablespoon herb and garlic seasoning
- 1 tablespoon soy sauce

- 1 tablespoon sesame oil
- 1 cup breadcrumbs
- ½ cup flour
- 1 eggs

PREPARATION

1. Season chicken with the following and set aside:

- 3 tablespoon herb and garlic seasoning
- 1 tablespoon soy sauce
- 1 tablespoon sesame oil
- 1 eggs

2. Toss breadcrumbs with flour and start coating your chicken with it.

3. Preheat Air Fryer to 375 F then lay out a layer of your popcorn chicken in cooking basket and cook for 15 minutes. Set timer. Once timer goes off shake the basket and cook for another 5 minutes. Repeat process for the next batch of popcorn chicken.

4. Serve with honey mustard and a side of curly fries.

Sriracha Fried Chicken Poppers

COOK TIME
15-20 MIN
PREP TIME
10 MIN
SERVINGS
4 SERVINGS

INGREDIENTS

- 4 pound chicken breasts cut into nugget size
- 1 tablespoon salt
- 4 tablespoon pepper

- 4 tablespoon Sriracha sauce
- 4 tablespoon honey
- 2 tablespoon dried parsley flakes

PREPARATION

1. In mixing bowl mix together all the above ingredients making sure that each nugget is coated with the sauce.

2. Preheat Air Fryer to 375 F then lay out the first layer of nuggets in cooking basket and cook for 15 minutes. Set timer.

3. Once timer goes off, shake basket and cook for another 5 minutes at 390 F.

   Serve with your favorite dipping sauce and a sprinkle of fresh pepper.

Notes

_____

_____

_____

_____

_____

_____

_____

_____

_____

Salt and Pepper Chicken Wings

COOK TIME
15-20 MIN
PREP TIME
10 MIN
SERVINGS
2-4 SERVINGS

INGREDIENTS

- 1 pound chicken wings
- 2-4 tablespoon of coarse salt
- 6 tablespoon pepper
- 2 tablespoon sesame oil
- Fresh lemon wedges for serving

PREPARATION

1. In mixing bowl mix together all the above ingredients not including the lemon wedges. Make sure each wing is coated with pepper, be generous with the pepper.

2. Preheat Air Fryer to 375 F then lay out the first layer of wings in cooking basket and cook for 15 minutes. Set timer.

3. Once timer goes off, shake basket or flip the wings over and cook again for another 5 minutes at 390 F.

4. Serve with fresh lemon wedges and a summer salad.

Notes

_____
_____
_____
_____
_____
_____
_____

Spicy Chicken Nuggets

COOK TIME
15-20 MIN
PREP TIME
10 MIN
SERVINGS
4 SERVINGS

INGREDIENTS

- 4 pound chicken breasts cut into nugget size
- 1 tablespoon salt
- 2 tablespoon Shichimi Powder (it's a Japanese Seasoning)
- 4 tablespoon Sriracha sauce
- 4 tablespoon Tabasco sauce (this adds a bit of a tart note to the sauce)
- 2 tablespoon chili oil
- 2 cups bread crumbs mixed with 2 tablespoons of chili flakes

PREPARATION

1. In mixing bowl mix together the following and set aside, make sure each nugget is coated with the sauce:
- 4 pound chicken breasts cut into nugget size
- 1 tablespoon salt
- 2 tablespoon Shichimi Powder (Japanese Seasoning)
- 4 tablespoon Sriracha sauce
- 4 tablespoon Tabasco sauce
- 2 tablespoon chili oil

2. Once everything is mixed add the in breadcrumb mixture and coat each nugget, it should become a "dry rub" for the nuggets.

3. Preheat Air Fryer to 375 F then lay out the first layer of nuggets in cooking basket and cook for 15 minutes. Set timer.

4. Once timer goes off, shake basket and cook for another 5 minutes at 390 F.

5. Repeat cooking process until all nuggets are cooked, serve with fresh celery sticks and cucumber slices.

Herbed Chicken Breast with Mustard Dressing

COOK TIME
15 MIN
PREP TIME
10 MIN
SERVINGS
4 SERVINGS

INGREDIENTS

- 2 medium size chicken breasts
- 1 tablespoon salt
- 2 tablespoon onion flakes
- 2 tablespoon dried oregano
- 2 tablespoon dried parsley flakes
- 2 tablespoon garlic powder
- 2 tablespoon sesame oil
- 1 bag of arugula greens

For the Mustard Dressing
- 1 cup Dijon
- 1 ½ cup sour cream
- 1 tablespoon honey
- 1 tablespoon sesame oil
- 1 tablespoon onion flakes
- Fresh cracked pepper and salt to taste
- 1 sprig of fresh green onion, finely sliced

PREPARATION

1. In mixing bowl mix together all the dry ingredients first, not including the chicken breasts and arugula greens. Once the spices are mixed coat your chicken breast with it and let it marinate for 5 minutes.

2. In another smaller mixing bowl mix together the Mustard Dressing ingredients and keep chilled before serving.

3. Preheat Air Fryer to 375 F and lay the chicken breasts in cooking basket and cook for 10 minutes. Set timer. Once timer goes off, flip the breasts and cook for another 5 minutes at 390 F. Set timer.

4. Once timer goes off, plate it on top of the arugula greens and serve with a dollop of the Mustard Dressing.

Beef Cuts

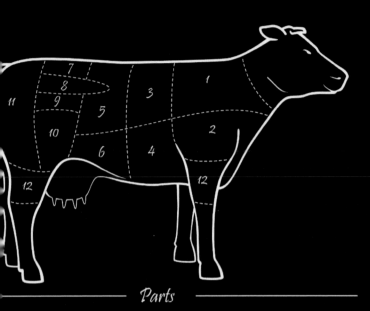

Parts

1 - Chuck   5 – Short Loin   9 - Top Sirloin
2 - Brisket   6 - Flank   10 - Bottom Sirloin
3 - Rib   7 – Sirloin   11 – Round
4 - Plate   8 - Tenderloin   12 – Shanks

Parts

1 – Chuck   5 – Short Loin   9 - Top Sir
2 - Brisket   6 - Flank   10 - Bottom
3 - Rib   7 - Sirloin   11 – Round
4. - Plate   8 - Tenderloin   12 – Shanks

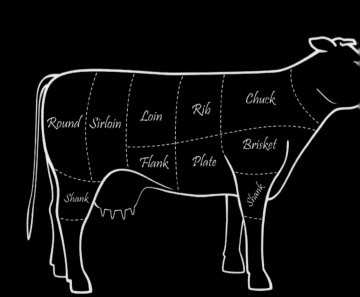

AIRFRYER

BEEF

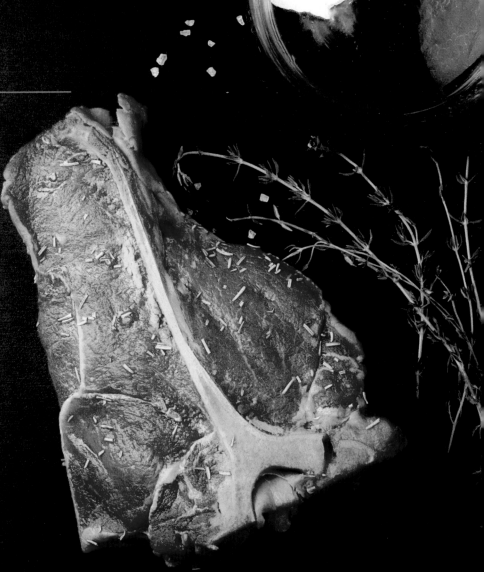

Ribeye Chimichurri Steak

COOK TIME
15 MIN
PREP TIME
15 MIN
SERVINGS
2 SERVINGS

*Please note this recipe is for 2 medium rare steaks cooked in the cooking basket.

INGREDIENTS

For the Steaks

- 2 medium size filets of sirloin steak
- Salt and pepper for seasoning
- 4 tablespoon of Worcestershire sauce
- 4 tablespoon of Dijon

For the Chimichurri

- In a medium bowl combine ½ cup of vinegar with 1 teaspoon of salt, garlic, shallot, oregano flakes and green Chile. Set aside.
- Loosely chop up a handful of cilantro and parsley.
- Use a fork, whisk in ¼ cup olive oil into the vinegar mixture along with the cilantro and parsley. Chill in fridge until serving.

PREPARATION

1. In mixing bowl season steak generously with salt and pepper then season with the rest of the steak ingredients.

2. Preheat Air Fryer to 390 F then lay the strips evenly in cooking basket and cook for 15 minutes. Set timer.

3. Once timer goes off, remove steak and serve immediately with Chimichurri sauce and frites

Crunchy Beef and Broccoli Egg Rolls

COOK TIME
15 MIN
PREP TIME
15 MIN
SERVINGS
6-10 EGG ROLLS

INGREDIENTS

- 1 package egg roll wrappers
- 1 egg
- 1 pound lean ground beef
- 1 onion, minced,
- 2 cloves of garlic, minced
- 4 cups of broccoli, finely chopped (only use the "flower" part of the broccoli)

- ½ cup celery, finally chopped
- 1 tablespoon soy sauce
- 2 tablespoon sesame oil
- 1-2 tablespoon salt
- 2 tablespoon white pepper
- 1 egg, beaten (this is used to seal the Egg Rolls)
- Olive oil for brushing

PREPARATION

1. In a large mixing bowl mix together all the ingredients, not including the egg roll wrappers, beaten egg, and olive oil. Heat up a large non-stick pan and sauté your beef mixture, with a drizzle of olive oil. It does not need to be fully cooked, about 80% cooked. Sauté on medium for 10-15 minutes.

2. Once the beef mixture is cooked begin rolling out your egg rolls. Place about ½ to 1 cup of mixture in center of wrapper and spread it out and fold forming rolls, seal the ends with the egg wash. Make sure you tuck the sides in before completing the roll. Repeat process until all your fillings are used. You should be able to make 6-10 egg rolls, depending on the size of your egg roll wrappers.

3. To cook the egg rolls, preheat Air Fryer to 200 F and begin to brush egg rolls with olive oil and lay them out evenly in cooking basket. Cook for 10 minutes. Set timer. Once timer goes off, rotate spring rolls and cook for another 5 minutes.

4. Serve with your favorite sweet and sour dipping sauce or your favorite stew.

Steak Poppers with Blue Cheese Sauce

COOK TIME
15 MIN
PREP TIME
15 MIN
SERVINGS
2 SERVINGS

INGREDIENTS

- 2 pound ribeye cut into bite sized chunks
- Salt and pepper for seasoning
- 1 tablespoon dried parsley flakes
- 4 tablespoon of Worcestershire sauce
- 4 tablespoon of Dijon

For the Blue Cheese Sauce

- Melt 25gram butter in a saucepan over a medium heat.
- Stir in 1 tablespoon of flour and slowly add ½ cup of cream, bring to simmer and keep stirring until smooth
- Slowly add in 50grams of chopped blue cheese and stir until combined.
- Add in some fresh chopped cilantro

PREPARATION

1. In large mixing bowl season steak chunks with a generous amount of salt and pepper along with the rest of the ingredients.

2. Preheat Air Fryer to 390 F then lay out a layer of the steak chunks in cooking basket and cook for 15 minutes.

3. This will give you medium rate steak bites. Set timer.

4. Once timer goes off remove and serve with a fresh arugula salad and blue cheese dipping sauce.

Country Fried Skirt Steak

COOK TIME
15 MIN
PREP TIME
10 MIN
SERVINGS
2 SERVINGS

INGREDIENTS

- 2 medium size filets of skirt steak
- 1 tablespoon sesame oil
- 1 tablespoon dried oregano flakes
- Salt and pepper for seasoning
- 4 tablespoon of Worcestershire sauce

- 4 tablespoon of Dijon
- 2 cup breadcrumbs
- ½ cup flour
- 2 eggs

PREPARATION

1. In a large bowl season skirt steak generously with salt and pepper and set aside.

2. Combine the following, then rub it evenly onto the skirt steaks, then set aside:
   - 1 tablespoon sesame oil
   - 1 tablespoon dried oregano flakes
   - Salt and pepper for seasoning
   - 4 tablespoon of Worcestershire sauce
   - 4 tablespoon of Dijon
   - 2 eggs

3. Combine breadcrumbs and flour and coat the steaks evenly on both sides.

4. Preheat Air Fryer to 390 F then lay out each steak in cooking basket and cook for 15 minutes. This will give you medium rate steak. Set timer.

5. Once timer goes off remove and serve with a side of jasmine rice and fried onions.

Crispy Beef Wontons

COOK TIME
15 MIN
PREP TIME
15-20 MIN
SERVINGS
2 SERVINGS

INGREDIENTS

- 1 package wonton sheets (you can purchase this at an Asian grocer)
- 1 pound lean ground beef
- 2 tablespoon sesame oil
- 2 tablespoon white pepper
- 2 tablespoon sea salt
- 1 teaspoon soy sauce
- 2 stalks green onion, finely chopped
- 1 carrot, finely chopped
- About ½ cup coriander leaves, finely chopped
- 2 gloves garlic, minced
- 1 Egg, beaten (to add to ground beef)
- 1 Egg, beaten (to seal the folded wonton sheets)
- Olive oil for brushing
- Silicone brush, to brush the egg wash over wontons

PREPARATION

1. In a large mixing bowl, mix the following ingredients:

- 1 pound lean ground beef
- 2 tablespoon sesame oil
- 2 tablespoon white pepper
- 2 tablespoon sea salt
- 1 teaspoon soy sauce
- 2 stalks green onion, finely chopped
- 1 carrot, finely chopped
- About ½ cup coriander leaves, finely chopped
- 2 gloves garlic, minced
- 1 Egg, beaten

2. Once well incorporated dust your countertop surface with some flour and begin to form your wontons. Keep making wontons until you run out of filling.

3. **To make the wontons:** Take some beef stuffing roughly 1-2 tablespoon size (this depends on the diameter of your wonton sheets) place the stuffing in the middle of the sheet, brush egg wash around the sheet and seal the edges in a crescent shape and pleat the edges (see photo). Repeat until all the filling is used up.

4. The Air Fryer basket fits roughly 10-15 wontons. For the rest of the wontons dust it with more flour and store in air tight container in the fridge for 2 days or in the freezer up to 2 weeks.

5. **To cook the wontons:** Preheat Air Fryer to 200 F and brush your wontons with olive oil and lay them evenly in cooking basket. Cook for 7 minutes. Set timer. Once timer goes off flip the wontons and cook for another 8 minutes. Serve hot with your favorite sweet and sour sauce and cucumber sticks.

Mini Eggs with the Works

COOK TIME
20 MIN
PREP TIME
10 MIN
SERVINGS
2 SERVINGS

INGREDIENTS

- 1 cup of ground beef
- 1 cup cherry tomatoes, sliced
- 4 large farm eggs
- 1 cup tomato sauce (choose your favorite)
- 1 cup beef stock

- 2 tablespoons sesame oil
- 2 tablespoons dried parsley flakes
- 2 teaspoon paprika
- 2 teaspoon chili flakes
- Salt and pepper to taste

PREPARATION

1. In mixing bowl marinate the ground beef with salt and pepper and the sesame oil. Divide them evenly between 2 small ceramic baking bowls. Then dived up the tomato sauce, cherry tomatoes, and beef stock between the two ceramic baking bowls and use a fork to combine the mixture.

2. Crack 2 large farm eggs in each ceramic bowl and sprinkle the paprika, parsley flakes and chili flakes.

3. Preheat Air Fryer to 350 F then lay the ceramic bowls in cooking basket and cook for 20 minutes. Set timer. Once timer goes off, remove carefully and serve with toast or a warm loaf of crusty baguette.

Roast Beef and Arugula Grilled Cheese

COOK TIME
10 MIN
PREP TIME
10 MIN
SERVINGS
2 SERVINGS

INGREDIENTS

- 6 slices of your favorite roast beef (for 2 sandwiches)
- 4 slices of sharp jack cheese
- 2 cups packed arugula (divided)
- Dijon for spreading

- Fresh cracked pepper and sea salt
- 4 slices of Italian Herb and Cheese Bread (choose your favorite)
- Pickles for serving

PREPARATION

1. To build your sandwich: Spread Dijon on all slices of bread, then spread better on the top side of the slices and then add couple cracks of fresh pepper and sea salt on the Dijon side of all 4 slices.

2. Begin to layer your sandwich in this order:
- On the first slice of bread add 1 slice of roast beef
- Arugula
- Jack cheese
- 1 slice of roast beef

- Arugula
- Jack cheese
- 1 slice of roast beef then sandwich it with slice of bread

3. Repeat this for the second sandwich. Preheat Air fryer 300 F and place both sandwiches into the cooking basket cook for 5 minutes. Set timer. Once timer goes off, flip it and cook for another 5 minutes. Set timer. Once timer goes off serve immediately with pickles and your favorite soup.

Beef Patty Steak Dinner

COOK TIME
25 MIN
PREP TIME
15 MIN
SERVINGS
4 SERVINGS

INGREDIENTS

- 1 pound of fresh ground beef from your butcher
- 2 tablespoon paprika
- 2 tablespoon red chili flakes
- 2 tablespoon sesame oil
- 2 tablespoon sea salt
- 1 tablespoon black pepper
- 1 tablespoon dried oregano
- 2 garlic cloves, minced
- 1 egg, whipped
- 400 grams green beans, ends trimmed and washed
- 4 tablespoons chili oil

PREPARATION

1. In mixing bowl toss the green beans with the chili oil and set aside.

2. In another mixing bowl marinate ground beef with paprika, chili flakes, sesame oil, salt and pepper, garlic, and oregano. Mix well, then add in the egg.

3. Start to form palm sized patties, you should be able to form 4 patties, store the extras in a container in your fridge.

4. Preheat the Air Fryer to 350 F, lay the green beans evenly over the cooking basket then lay 2 of the patties on top of the cooking basket and cook for 20 minutes. Set timer.

5. Once timer goes off, carefully flip the patties and cook for another 5 minutes. Set timer, once timer goes off serve immediately with your favorite rich or pasta.

Avocado Meatball Boat

COOK TIME
15 MIN
PREP TIME
10 MIN
SERVINGS
2 SERVINGS

INGREDIENTS

- ½ pound ground beef
- 1 shallot, minced
- 2 tablespoon sesame oil
- 2 tablespoon dried oregano
- 2 tablespoon dried parsley flakes
- 2 tablespoon sea salt
- 2 tablespoon white pepper
- 4 tablespoon Worcestershire sauce
- 2 ripe avocados pitted, and cut in half (this is the "boat" where you will place your meatballs in)

PREPARATION

1. Take your avocado halves and scoop out some of the flesh so that it will fit a golf ball sized meat ball in the middle.

2. In a mixing bowl mix the ground beef with the extra avocado flesh and then add the shallot, sesame oil, oregano, parsley flakes, salt and pepper and the Worcestershire sauce. Mix well. Form 4 golf ball sized meatballs and place them into your avocado boat.

3. Preheat Air Fryer to 350 F and lay the 4 avocado boats into the cooking basket and cook for 15 minutes. Set timer. Once timer goes off, poke a knife into the meatball to make sure it's cooked, add another 5 minutes if it's still pink inside.

4. Serve with fresh cracked pepper and crusty baguette.

Stuffed Portobello Mushroom Caps

COOK TIME
15 MIN
PREP TIME
10 MIN
SERVINGS
2 SERVINGS

INGREDIENTS

- 2 large Portobello mushroom caps, washed and pat dried
- 1 cup ground beef
- 1 cup grated sharp white cheddar
- ½ cup green peppers, finely chopped

- 1 garlic clove, minced
- 2 tablespoon sea salt
- 1 tablespoon pepper
- 1 tablespoons sesame oil
- 1 tablespoon dried parsley flakes

PREPARATION

1. In mixing bowl, mix together the ground beef with all the ingredients. Set aside.

2. Use a bit of olive oil and grease the bottom of the mushroom caps, and then spoon the beef mixture into the 2 Portobello mushroom caps.

Try not to over stuff it and break the side walls of the mushroom caps.

3. Preheat Air fryer to 350 F and place your mushroom caps into the booking basket. Cook for 15 minutes and set timer. Once timer goes off, serve with a side of fresh green salad.

Pork Cuts

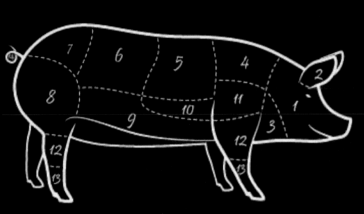

Parts

1 - Head	6 - Loin	11 - Arm schoulder
2 - Ear	7 - Rump	12 - Hocks
3 - Jowl	8 - Leg / Ham	13 - Feets / Trotters
4 - Shoulder	9 - Belly / Bacon	14 - Tale
5 - Rack	10 - Spare Ribs	

Parts

1 - Head	6 - Loin	11 - Arm schoulder
2 - Ear	7 - Rump	12 - Hocks
3 - Jowl	8 - Leg / Ham	13 - Feets / Trot
4 - Shoulder	9 - Belly / Bacon	14 - Tale
5 - Rack	10 - Spare Ribs	

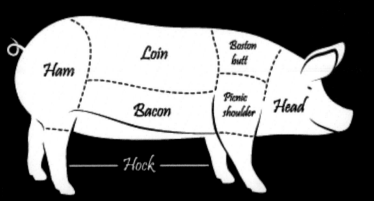

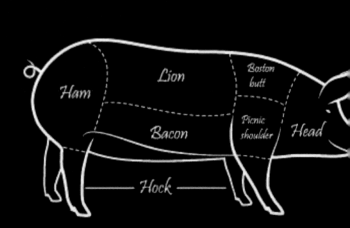

AIRFRYER

PORK

Buttermilk Fried Pork Chops

COOK TIME
15 MIN
PREP TIME
10 MIN
SERVINGS
2 SERVINGS

INGREDIENTS

- 2 pieces of medium size bone-in pork chop
- Salt and pepper for seasoning
- 2 tablespoon sesame oil
- 1 tablespoon dried onion flakes
- 1 tablespoon dried oregano flakes

- 1 cup butter milk
- 2 cup breadcrumbs
- 1 cup flour
- 1 eggs

PREPARATION

1. In a large bowl season pork chops generously with salt and pepper and set aside.

2. In another smaller bowl whisk together the eggs and buttermilk with sesame oil, onion flakes, and oregano flakes.

3. Combine breadcrumbs and flour.

4. Dip your pork chops into buttermilk egg mixture and then coat with breadcrumb mixture evenly on both sides.

5. Preheat Air Fryer to 375 F then lay out each pork chop in cooking basket and cook for 15 minutes. Set timer.

6. Once timer goes off cook for another 5 minutes at 390 F.

7. Serve with lemon wedges and fresh salad on the side.

Sourdough Prosciutto Grilled Cheese

COOK TIME
10-15 MIN
PREP TIME
10 MIN
SERVINGS
2 SERVINGS

INGREDIENTS

- 4 slices of sourdough (you can use practically any type of bread) This recipe is designed to fit 2 sandwiches inside the cooking basket
- 4 slices of sharp Monterey Jack cheese (choose your favorite)

- 4 slices of Prosciutto
- Small handful of arugula
- Butter
- Fresh cracked pepper to taste

PREPARATION

1. Butter both sides of the sourdough generously, then add a crack of pepper onto each slice of sourdough. **Begin your layers in this order:**
- Monterey Jack Cheese
- Arugula
- 2 slices of Prosciutto
- Monterey Jack Cheese

2. Preheat Air Fryer to 300 F and lay the two sandwiches side by side and cook for 5 minutes. Set timer. Once timer goes off, flip the sandwiches and cook for another 5 minutes.

3. Serve with a side of pickles and your favorite tomato soup.

Notes

_____
_____
_____
_____
_____
_____
_____

Herbed Pork Chops

COOK TIME
15-20 MIN
PREP TIME
10 MIN
SERVINGS
2 SERVINGS

INGREDIENTS

- 2 pieces of medium size bone-in pork chop
- 1 tablespoon salt
- 2 tablespoon pepper
- 4 tablespoon of dried rosemary
- 4 tablespoons of dried thyme

- 4 tablespoons of dried sage
- 1 tablespoon dried onion flakes
- 1 tablespoon dried oregano flakes
- 4 tablespoon of melted butter sesame oil
- 1 tablespoon sesame oil

PREPARATION

1. In a large mix together all the dry ingredients with the butter and sesame oil, then coat each side of your pork chops evenly.

2. Preheat Air Fryer to 375 F then lay the pork chops evenly in cooking basket and cook for 15 minutes. Set timer.

3. Once timer goes off, flip pork chops and cook at 390 F for another 5 minutes.

4. Serve with a side of saffron rice or steamed green beans.

Notes

_____
_____
_____
_____
_____

Smoked Montreal Dry Rub Pork Ribs

COOK TIME
30 MIN
PREP TIME
15 MIN
SERVINGS
2-4 SERVINGS

INGREDIENTS

- 1 pound of pork ribs, washed and pat dry

- **For the Dry Rub** (you can use this rub for other meats or seafood)
- ½ cup salt
- 2 tablespoon black pepper

- 1tablespoon crushed red pepper
- 1 tablespoon dried thyme
- 1 tablespoon dried rosemary
- 1 tablespoon dried fennel seeds
- 2 tablespoon onion powder
- ½ tablespoon garlic powder

PREPARATION

1. In a large mixing bowl combine the ribs with the Dry Rub making sure it's well coated.

2. Preheat Air Fryer 350 F and layer the ribs into cooking basket and cook for 15 minutes. Set timer. Once timer goes off turn the ribs with a set of tongs and cook for another 15 minutes. Set timer.

3. Once timer goes off serve the ribs with fresh cucumber and celery sticks with your favorite dipping sauce.

Notes

_____
_____
_____
_____
_____
_____
_____
_____
_____

Ground Pork Poppers

COOK TIME
15 MIN
PREP TIME
10 MIN
SERVINGS
2-4 SERVINGS

INGREDIENTS

- 1 pound of ground lean pork
- 1 clove garlic, minced
- ½ green pepper diced into very small pieces
- 2 tablespoon pepper

- 2 tablespoon coarse salt
- 1 tablespoon dried onion flakes
- 1 tablespoon dried oregano flakes
- 1 tablespoon sesame oil

PREPARATION

1. In a large mixing bowl, mix the above ingredients and start forming small bite sized balls "poppers"

2. Preheat Air Fryer to 375 F then lay out the first layers of the ground pork poppers evenly in the cooking basket and cook for 15 minutes. Set timer.

3. Once timer goes off, repeat the process until all your poppers are cooked.

4. Serve with your favorite pasta or in warm dinner rolls with spicy tomato sauce and shredded cheddar cheese

Notes

_____

_____

_____

_____

Sockeye Salmon Cuts

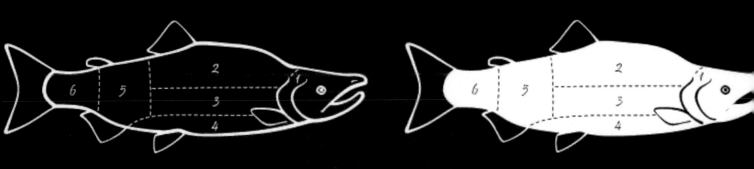

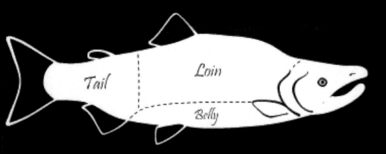

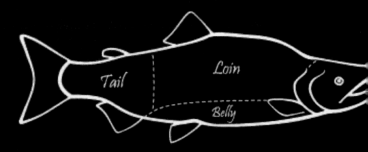

AIRFRYER
SEAFOOD

Popcorn Shrimp

COOK TIME
15 MIN
PREP TIME
10 MIN
SERVINGS
4 SERVINGS

INGREDIENTS

- 2-3 pounds medium size shrimp, thawed and peeled
- 1 tablespoon salt
- 2 tablespoon pepper
- 2 tablespoon sesame oil

- 2 cup panko crumbs (Panko is a Japanese style breadcrumbs)
- 1 cup breadcrumbs
- ½ cup flour
- 3 eggs

PREPARATION

1. In a large mixing bowl, beat the 3 eggs, with sesame oil, then add the salt, and pepper and whisk until mixed. Add in the shrimp and coat it evenly with the egg mixture. Set aside.

2. In another large mixing bowl toss together the panko, regular breadcrumbs and flour. Add in another pinch of salt and pepper.

3. Use a strainer to drain the shrimp mixture from the egg mixture. Toss the shrimp into the panko breadcrumbs and coat the wet shrimp evenly.

4. Preheat Air Fryer to 375 F then lay the first layer of the popcorn shrimp in cooking basket and cook for 5 minutes. Set timer. Once timer goes off, give it a shake, set timer for another 10 minutes. Once timer goes off, repeat process until all the shrimp is cooked.

5. Serve with fresh celery sticks, lemon wedges, and your favorite dipping sauce.

Sake Seafood Fry

COOK TIME
20 MIN
PREP TIME
20 MIN
SERVINGS
2 SERVINGS

INGREDIENTS

- ½ pound of fresh Manila Clams
- ½ pound of mussels
- ½ pound of fresh prawns
- Juice of 2 medium size lemon
- 2 cup Japanese Sake (or rice wine)

- 2 tablespoon sea salt
- 1 tablespoon dried parsley flakes
- 1 tablespoon onion flakes
- 2 tablespoon sesame oil

PREPARATION

1. Scrub and clean the clams and mussels then let it soak in a bowl of cold water for 10 minutes, this will allow it to release any sand in the clams and mussels. Clean prawns under cold running water and set aside.

2. In another large mixing bowl whisk together the wet and dry ingredients. Drain clams, mussels, prawns and add it to the mixing bowl and let it soak in the mixture for another 10 minutes.

3. Preheat Air fryer to 350 F, drain all liquid from the seafood and layer the seafood into the cooking basket in this order: Mussels/Clams/Prawns. Cook for 10 minutes. Set timer. Once timer goes off, increase temperature to 370 F and cook for another 10 minutes.

4. Once timer goes off check that all the shells are fully opened. Serve with lemon wedges on the side.

Salmon Fish and Chips

COOK TIME
15-25 MIN
PREP TIME
15 MIN
SERVINGS
2 SERVINGS

INGREDIENTS

The fish
- 2 medium size salmon filets
- 4 tablespoon salt & white pepper, mixed
- 2 tablespoon sesame oil
- 2 cup panko crumbs
- 1 cup breadcrumbs mixed with ½ cup flour
- 2 eggs

The chips
- 2 large potatoes, thinly sliced into chip slices
- 1 tablespoon salt
- 2 tablespoon white pepper
- 1 tablespoon sesame oil

PREPARATION

1. In large mixing bowl, whisk together the eggs, sesame oil, salt and pepper and soak each of the cod filet in the egg mixture. Set aside.

2. In another large mixing bowl toss the chip slices with the sesame oil, salt and pepper until evenly coated.

3. Mix the panko, breadcrumbs and flour in another mixing bowl, then coat each cod filet with the panko mixture.

4. Preheat Air Fryer to 375 F and lay the fish filet evenly in cooking basket and cook for 10 minutes. Set timer. Once timer goes off flip the fish and cook for another 5 minutes. Plate it.

5. Then add your potatoes slices and cook for 10 minutes, or until desired crispiness. Serve with tartar sauce and fresh green salad.

Summer Salmon and Dill

COOK TIME
15 MIN
PREP TIME
10 MIN
SERVINGS
2 SERVINGS

INGREDIENTS

- 2 fresh salmon filets
- 2 tablespoons soy sauce
- 2 tablespoons sea salt
- 2 tablespoon white pepper

- 4 tablespoons dried dill
- 2 springs of fresh dill
- 2 tablespoon sesame oil
- 4 slices of fresh lemon

PREPARATION

1. In mixing bowl whisk together, soy, sea salt, white pepper, dill flakes, and sesame oil. Marinate the salmon filets in the mixture. Set aside for 5 minutes.

2. Preheat Air Fryer to 375 F then lay the salmon evenly in cooking basket and lay 2 a sprig of fresh dill on each fish then lay the slices of lemon on top of the fresh dill and cook for 15 minutes. Set timer.

3. Once timer goes off, serve the salmon over a bread of fresh salad greens with fresh cracked pepper.

Notes

Crispy Fish Sticks

COOK TIME
15-20 MIN
PREP TIME
15 MIN
SERVINGS
4 SERVINGS

INGREDIENTS

- 2 pounds fresh halibut cut into sticks
- 1 tablespoon salt
- 2 tablespoon white pepper
- 2 tablespoon dried parsley flakes
- 2 tablespoon soy sauce

- 1 tablespoon sesame oil
- 2 cups panko mixed with 1 cup seasoned breadcrumbs
- ½ cup flour
- 2 eggs

PREPARATION

1. In large mixing bowl coat the fish sticks with the sesame oil, soy sauce, salt, white pepper and dried parsley flakes. Once all mixed, coat the fish with the flour.

2. In another bowl beat the eggs and dip the fish sticks into the egg and then coat it in the panko breadcrumb mix and lay it on a flat sheet of wax paper. Repeat the process until all the fish sticks is coated and breaded.

3. Preheat Air Fryer to 370 F then lay the fish sticks evenly in cooking basket and cook for 10 minutes. Set timer. Once timer goes off, shake basket, and then cook for another 5 minutes. Repeat until everything is cooked.

4. Serve with a chili tartar sauce and fresh sliced cucumber.

Spicy Cajun Shrimp

COOK TIME
15 MIN
PREP TIME
10 MIN
SERVINGS
2 SERVINGS

INGREDIENTS

- 2 pound jumbo shrimp, thawed and peeled
- 1 tablespoon salt
- 2 tablespoon pepper
- 2 tablespoon paprika
- 1 teaspoon garlic powder
- 1 teaspoon dried oregano
- 2 tablespoon sesame oil
- 1 tablespoon chili oil

PREPARATION

1. In large mixing bowl, mix together the above ingredients. Make sure each shrimp is coated in the seasoning.

2. Preheat Air Fryer to 375 F then lay the shrimps evenly in cooking basket and cook for 15 minutes. Set timer.

3. Once timer goes off, serve with a side of jasmine rice and fresh grilled root vegetables.

Notes

_____

_____

_____

_____

_____

_____

_____

_____

_____

Not-so-old-fashion Fried Scallops

COOK TIME
15 MIN
PREP TIME
10 MIN
SERVINGS
2 SERVINGS

INGREDIENTS

- 2 pound frozen scallops, thawed
- 1 tablespoon salt
- 2 tablespoon white pepper
- 1 tablespoon garlic powder
- 4 tablespoon red pepper flakes

- 1 teaspoon finely grated lemon zest
- 1 tablespoon sesame oil
- 2 cup panko crumbs
- 1 cup breadcrumbs mixed with ½ cup flour
- 2 eggs

PREPARATION

1. In large mixing bowl, marinate the scallops with salt, white pepper, garlic powder, red pepper flakes, and sesame oil and lemon zest. Set aside.

2. In another mixing bowl mix the panko and breadcrumbs together.

3. Whisk the egg and dip each scallop in egg then coat it with the panko mixture, repeat until all scallops are coated with panko mixture.

4. Preheat Air Fryer to 370 F then lay the scallops in cooking basket and cook for 15 minutes. Set timer.

5. Once timer goes off, serve over a bed of fresh arugula and honey mustard dressing.

Ahi Tuna Poppers

COOK TIME
15 MIN
PREP TIME
10 MIN
SERVINGS
2 SERVINGS

INGREDIENTS

- 1 pound of fresh tuna steak, cut into bite sized chunks
- 2 tablespoon sea salt
- 4 tablespoon sesame oil
- 1 cup panko
- ½ cup toasted sesame seeds
- ½ cup flour

PREPARATION

1. In large mixing bowl, marinate the tuna chunks with sesame oil and sea salt. Set aside.

2. In another mixing bowl mix together the panko, sesame seeds and flour. Cover each piece of tuna with the panko mixture. Make sure it's evenly covered.

3. Preheat Air Fryer to 375 F and lay the tuna chunks in cooking basket and cook for 15 minutes. Set timer. Once timer goes off give the basket a shake and cook for another 5 minutes. Set timer.

4. Once timer goes off, serve with a bit of Japanese soy sauce and fresh green scallions.

Notes

_____
_____
_____
_____
_____
_____
_____
_____

Savory Crab Cakes

COOK TIME
15 MIN
PREP TIME
15 MIN
SERVINGS
4 SERVINGS

INGREDIENTS

- 1 pound of shredded crab meat (you can purchase this from your local seafood grocer or in the frozen isle of most supermarkets. If you cannot find any, use frozen imitation crab sticks and thaw before shredding.)
- 1 cup packed shredded cooked chicken breasts
- ¼ cup green onion thinly sliced
- ¼ cup chives thinly sliced
- 1 large egg

- 2 tablespoon Dijon
- ½ cup light mayonnaise
- 1 tablespoon salt
- 2 tablespoon pepper
- 1 tablespoon sesame oil
- 1 cup panko
- 2 cup breadcrumbs
- ½ cup flour

PREPARATION

1. In large mixing bowl mix the crab meat and chicken with the above ingredients not including the panko, breadcrumbs, and flour. Once well mixed form "cake" patties, roughly the size of your palm (this should give you about 4 crab cakes.)

2. In another bowl mix together the panko, breadcrumbs, and flour. Then coat each crab cake with the panko mixture.

3. Preheat Air Fryer to 370 F then lay the crab cakes into the cooking basket, you should be able to fit all 4 cakes. Cook for 8 minutes. Set timer. Once timer goes off, flip each cake and cook for another 8 minutes.

4. Serve over a bed of fresh arugula with tartar on the side for dipping.

AIRFRYER

VEGETABLES

Mama's Fried Brussels Sprouts

COOK TIME
20-25 MIN
PREP TIME
10 MIN
SERVINGS
4 SERVINGS

INGREDIENTS

- 1 pound of Brussels sprouts
- ½ cup of parmesan powder
- 2 tablespoon olive oil
- 1 tablespoon sesame oil
- 1 tablespoon salt
- 1 tablespoon white pepper

PREPARATION

1. In large mixing bowl, mix the Brussels sprouts with the above ingredients. Make sure each Brussels sprouts is coated with the seasoning and parmesan powder.

2. Preheat Air Fryer to 375 F then add all the Brussels sprouts to cooking basket and cook for 15 minutes. Set timer. Once timer goes off shake the basket. And cook for another 10 minutes.

3. Serve with your favorite protein and jasmine rice.

Notes

_____
_____
_____
_____
_____
_____
_____
_____
_____
_____
_____

Parmesan Fried Cauliflower

COOK TIME
15 MIN
PREP TIME
10 MIN
SERVINGS
4 SERVINGS

INGREDIENTS

- 1 head cauliflower chopped in bite sized chunks
- ¼ cup parmesan powder
- 2 tablespoon dried parsley flakes

- 1 tablespoon salt
- 2 tablespoon white pepper
- 1 tablespoon sesame oil

PREPARATION

1. In a large mixing bowl toss the cauliflower with the above ingredients until the cauliflower chunks are well coated.

2. Preheat Air Fryer to 370 F then add the cauliflower into the cooking basket and cook for 10 minutes.

3. Set timer. Once timer goes off shake the basket and then cook at 390 F for another 5 minutes. Set timer.

4. Once timer goes off, plate it and serve with your favorite pasta.

Notes

Toasted Sesame Seed Kale

COOK TIME
10-15 MIN
PREP TIME
10 MIN
SERVINGS
2 SERVINGS

INGREDIENTS

- 1 bunch of kale
- 1½ tablespoon sea salt
- 1 tablespoon olive oil

- 2 tablespoon sesame oil
- ½ table spoon red chili flakes
- Toasted sesame seeds for garnish

PREPARATION

1. Remove and discard thick stock and roughly chop the leaves. Was in cold water and pat dry with clean towel or paper towels.

2. In large mixing bowl toss the kale with the sea salt, olive oil, sesame oil and chili flakes

3. Preheat Air Fryer to 350 F then layer the kale in cooking basket and cook for 10-15 minutes (until crispy.) Set timer.

4. Once timer goes off, serve the kale with your favorite tomato soup and grilled cheese.

Notes

_____
_____
_____
_____
_____
_____
_____

Crispy Zucchini Sticks

COOK TIME
15-20 MIN
PREP TIME
10 MIN
SERVINGS
2-4 SERVINGS

INGREDIENTS

- 3 medium zucchini sliced into sticks
- 2 eggs, beaten
- ½ cup breadcrumbs
- ½ cup panko

- 1 tablespoon salt
- 1 tablespoon white pepper
- 2 tablespoon Parmesan cheese powder
- ½ tablespoon garlic powder

PREPARATION

1. In large mixing bowl, mix together all the dry ingredients not including the beaten eggs.

2. In another mixing bowl mix together the zucchini sticks with the eggs, and then coat each stick with the panko and breadcrumbs mixture.

3. Preheat Air Fryer to 375 F and lay the zucchini sticks evenly in cooking basket and cook for 15-20 minutes. Set timer.

4. Once timer goes off serve with ranch or marinara dipping sauce along with the fried fish sticks.

Notes

_____
_____
_____
_____
_____
_____
_____
_____
_____
_____

Garlicky Fried Bok Choy

COOK TIME
15 MIN
PREP TIME
10 MIN
SERVINGS
4 SERVINGS

INGREDIENTS

- ½ pound of baby bok choy, washed and pat dry
- 2 tablespoon sea salt
- 2 tablespoon white pepper
- 3 tablespoon garlic powder
- 3 tablespoon sesame oil

PREPARATION

1. In large mixing bowl, toss the baby bok coy with the above ingredients. Make sure the leaves are well coated with the seasoning and oil.

2. Preheat Air Fryer to 375 F then lay the baby bok choy evenly in cooking basket and cook for 10 minutes. Set timer. Once timer goes off. Shake basket and cook for another 5 minutes.

3. Once timer goes off serve with your favorite fried rice or homemade stew.

Notes

_____

_____

_____

_____

_____

_____

_____

_____

Chili Oil Green Beans

COOK TIME
20 MIN
PREP TIME
10 MIN
SERVINGS
2 SERVINGS

INGREDIENTS

- 1 pound of long green beans with ends trimmed
- 1 tablespoon sea salt
- 2 tablespoon Sriracha sauce
- 3 tablespoon chili oil
- 1 tablespoon sesame oil

PREPARATION

1. In large mixing bowl toss the green beans with the above ingredients making sure each been is well coated.

2. Preheat Air Fryer to 370 F then lay beans evenly in layers in cooking basket and cook for 25 minutes. Set timer.

3. Once timer goes off. Serve the Chili Oil Green Beans with your favorite fried rice or stew.

Notes

Crinkle Fries Poutine

COOK TIME
25 MIN
PREP TIME
10 MIN
SERVINGS
2-4 SERVINGS

INGREDIENTS

- 1 pound of your favorite crinkle fries (your favorite frozen brand)
- 4 tablespoons sea salt
- 4 tablespoons onion flakes
- 4 tablespoons garlic powder
- ½ can beef stock
- 1 cup of hoisin sauce
- 1 cup heavy cream
- ½ cup melted butter
- 2 cups shredded cheddar

PREPARATION

1. In a small saucepan heat up the beef stock over medium. Once it's simmering, add the hoisin sauce, heavy cream and butter. Stir until incorporated (2-5 minutes). Keep stirring and add a pinch of salt and pepper to taste. Take it off the heat and set aside.

2. In a large mixing bowl and season your crinkle fries with sea salt, onion flakes, and garlic powder

3. Preheat Air Fryer to 370 F then add crinkle fries to cooking basket and cook for 20 minutes. Set timer. Once timer goes off shake basket and cook at 390 F for another 5 minutes.

4. Once timer goes off, divide in deep bowl, pour the gravy and sprinkle with shredded cheddar.

Tater-Tot Chili

COOK TIME
15 MIN
PREP TIME
20 MIN
SERVINGS
2-4 SERVINGS

INGREDIENTS

- 1 pound tater-tots
- 1 cup shredded cheddar

For the Chili
- 1 pound ground beef
- 1 onion chopped

- 1 tomato diced
- 2 cloves garlic, minced
- 1 can of your favorite cooked beans
- 2 tablespoon chili oil
- 1 tablespoon salt
- 1 tablespoon chili flakes

PREPARATION

1. In a large bowl, season the ground beef with the salt, chili oil, garlic, and chili flakes.

2. Preheat Air Fryer to 375 F and add the tater-tots to cooking basket and cook for 15 minutes. Set timer.

3. In a large sauce pan, drizzle some olive oil and sauté the onion and tomatoes over medium for 2 minutes, and then add in the beef and cook until all cooked.

4. Add in the canned beans into the beef mixture and cook on high for 5 minutes, constantly stirring. Add salt and pepper to taste. Turn off the heat and set aside.

5. Once timer goes off for the Air Fryer, plate the tater-tots in a deep bowl, layer a ladle of the chili over the tater-tots and serve with shredded cheddar.

All Dressed Potato Wedges

COOK TIME
25 MIN
PREP TIME
10 MIN
SERVINGS
2 SERVINGS

INGREDIENTS

- 2 large potatoes peeled and cut into wedges
- 3 tablespoon salt
- 3 tablespoon white pepper
- 2 tablespoon garlic powder
- 2 tablespoon olive oil
- ½ cup white vinegar

PREPARATION

1. In large mixing bowl coat the potato wedges with the above ingredients, making sure each wedge is coated evenly.

2. Preheat Air Fryer to 375 F then lay the wedges evenly in cooking basket and cook for 20 minutes.

3. Set timer. Once timer goes off shake basket and cook at 390F for another 5 minutes. Set timer.

4. Once timer goes off serve with a garden salad and ranch dipping sauce.

Notes

Deep Fried Pickles

COOK TIME
15 MIN
PREP TIME
10 MIN
SERVINGS
2 SERVINGS

INGREDIENTS

- 6 large pickles (choose your favorite brand)
- 1 tablespoon salt
- 2 tablespoon pepper
- 2 cups panko
- 1 cup breadcrumbs
- ½ cup flour
- 2 eggs

PREPARATION

1. In bowl, season pickles with salt and pepper then dust it with the flour.

2. Beat the eggs, and in another large mixing bowl toss together the panko, and breadcrumbs.

3. Take each pickle and dip into the egg, and then coat it with the panko mixture. Repeat until all 6 pickles are coated.

4. Preheat Air Fryer to 375 F then lay the pickles evenly in cooking basket and cook for 15 minutes. Set timer.

5. Once timer goes off, serve with your favorite chili dog and fresh cucumber salad.

Notes

_____
_____
_____
_____
_____
_____
_____
_____

Skinny Yam Fries

COOK TIME
25 MIN
PREP TIME
10 MIN
SERVINGS
2 SERVINGS

INGREDIENTS

- 2 large orange yams, peeled and cut into skinny fries
- 1 tablespoon salt
- 2 tablespoon white pepper
- 2 tablespoon honey
- 2 tablespoon sesame oil

PREPARATION

1. In large mixing bowl toss the yam fries with the above ingredients making sure each fry is coated evenly.

2. Preheat Air Fryer to 375 F then lay the yam fries evenly in cooking basket and cook for 15 minutes.

3. Set timer. Once timer goes off, shake basket and cook for another 10 minutes. Set timer.

4. Once timer goes off, serve with your favorite dipping sauce and a fresh fruit salad.

Notes

_____

_____

_____

_____

_____

_____

_____

_____

_____

_____

_____

Breaded Cucumber Sticks

COOK TIME
15 MIN
PREP TIME
10 MIN
SERVINGS
2-4 SERVINGS

INGREDIENTS

- 2 large cucumbers washed, and cut evenly into sticks (about 4 inches long)
- 1 tablespoon salt
- 2 tablespoon white pepper
- 2 tablespoon garlic powder
- 2 tablespoon sesame oil
- 1 egg
- 2 cups panko
- 1 cup breadcrumbs
- 1 cup flour

PREPARATION

1. In mixing bowl whisk together the egg with salt, white pepper, garlic powder, and sesame oil. Toss the cucumber sticks with the mixture until it is all coated.

2. In another large mixing bowl toss together the panko, breadcrumbs, and flour.

3. Take a pair of tongs and transfer each stick of cucumber into panko mixture and toss until the cucumber sticks are well coated.

4. Preheat Air Fryer to 375 F then lay the cucumber sticks evenly in cooking basket and cook for 15 minutes. Set timer. Once timer goes off serve with your favorite pasta or chili dogs.

Notes

_____

_____

_____

_____

_____

_____

_____

_____

Parsley Baked Potatoes

COOK TIME
35-40 MIN
PREP TIME
10 MIN
SERVINGS
2 SERVINGS

INGREDIENTS

- 2 medium sized potatoes for baking
- 2 tablespoons sesame oil
- 1 tablespoon salt
- 2 tablespoon garlic powder
- 2 tablespoon dried parsley flakes

PREPARATION

1. Wash potatoes and poke "air holes" with a fork around your potatoes. Brush them with sesame oil.

2. Then mix together your dry ingredients and sprinkle it over your potatoes.

3. Preheat Air Fryer 390 F and place your potatoes in cooking basket and cook for 35-40 minutes. Set timer. Cook until tender when poked with a fork.

4. Serve with sour cream and your favorite protein or stew.

Notes

_____
_____
_____
_____
_____
_____
_____
_____
_____
_____
_____
_____
_____

Roasted Garlic Fried Broccoli

COOK TIME
15 MIN
PREP TIME
10 MIN
SERVINGS
4 SERVINGS

INGREDIENTS

- 1-2 heads of broccoli, washed and cut into bite sized chunks
- 1 tablespoon salt
- 2 tablespoon pepper

- 3 tablespoon garlic powder
- 2 tablespoon onion flakes
- 2 tablespoon sesame oil

PREPARATION

1. In large mixing bowl, toss the broccoli chunks with the above ingredients. Make sure each broccoli chunk is well coated.

2. Preheat Air Fryer to 375 F then distribute the broccoli chunks evenly in cooking basket and cook for 15 minutes. Set timer.

3. Once timer goes off, serve on platter with ranch dipping sauce or a blue cheese sauce.

Notes

_____

_____

_____

_____

_____

_____

_____

_____

_____

_____

Refresh with Fruit Infused Water

Fruit for Thought

The best way to make flavored water is with a large juice pitcher and layer it with ice and fruits. The following fruit infused water recipes are designed to make 1 pitcher of water.

This will be ideal for a family that wish to drink more water with their dinner meals, instead of sugary juices and sodas. I would recommend keeping the flavored water for no more than 2 days, it is best to be consumed while it's fresh.

Thirsty gal,
Kelly Cohen

Strawberry Infused Water

Strawberry Basil Lemon Water

INGREDIENTS

- 10 strawberries, sliced
- ½ lemon, sliced
- 5-10 leaves of fresh basil (depends on leaf size, if smaller use 10 leaves)

PREPARATION

- In a large juice pitcher, layer the ingredients with cubes of ice.
- Add fresh filtered water, and keep in fridge before serving.

Strawberry Mint and Raw Honey Water

INGREDIENTS

- 10 strawberries, sliced
- ½ Raw Honey dissolved in warm water (DO NOT use boiling water)
- 5-10 leaves of fresh mint (depends on leaf size, if smaller use 10 leaves)

PREPARATION

- In a large juice pitcher fill it halfway with cubes of ice and fresh filtered water, and then stir in the Raw Honey water.
- Add in the strawberry slices and mint and more cubes of ice and filtered water. Keep in fridge before serving.

Notes

_____
_____
_____
_____
_____
_____

Strawberry Kiwi Lime Water

INGREDIENTS

- 10 strawberries, sliced
- 1 kiwi, peeled and sliced
- 1 small lime sliced

PREPARATION

- In a large juice pitcher, layer the ingredients with cubes of ice.
- Add fresh filtered water, and keep in fridge before serving.

Very Berry Water and Cucumbers

INGREDIENTS

- 8 strawberries, sliced
- ½ cup fresh raspberries
- ½ cup frozen blackberries
- 6 cucumber slices

PREPARATION

- In a large juice pitcher, layer the ingredients with cubes of ice.
- Add fresh filtered water, and keep in fridge before serving.

Strawberry Cucumber with Rose Petals

INGREDIENTS

- 10 strawberries, sliced
- 6 cucumber slices
- ¼ cup dried rose petals

PREPARATION

- In a large juice pitcher, layer the ingredients with cubes of ice.
- Add fresh filtered water, and keep in fridge before serving.

Strawberry Pineapple Mint Water

INGREDIENTS

- 6 strawberries, sliced
- 6 slices of pineapple (if using canned, make sure liquid is drained)
- 5-10 leaves of fresh basil (depends on leaf size, is smaller use 10 leaves)

PREPARATION

- In a large juice pitcher, layer the ingredients with cubes of ice.
- Add fresh filtered water, and keep in fridge before serving.

Blueberry Infused Water

Blueberry Kiwi Lavender Water

INGREDIENTS

- 1 cup blueberries
- 1 kiwi peeled and sliced
- 1 spring of dried lavender

PREPARATION

- In a large juice pitcher, layer the ingredients with cubes of ice.
- Add fresh filtered water, and keep in fridge before serving.

Blueberry Lychee Mint Water

INGREDIENTS

- 1 cup blueberries
- 1 can of lychee, drained
- 5-10 leaves of fresh mint (depends on leaf size, if smaller use 10 leaves)

PREPARATION

- In a large juice pitcher, layer the ingredients with cubes of ice.
  Add fresh filtered water, and keep in fridge before serving.

Blueberry and White Peach with Lavender Water

INGREDIENTS

- 1 cup blueberries
- 1 white peach peeled and sliced
- 1 spring of dried lavender

PREPARATION

- In a large juice pitcher, layer the ingredients with cubes of ice.
- Add fresh filtered water, and keep in fridge before serving.

Blueberry Pomegranate Rose Water

INGREDIENTS

- 1 cup blueberries
- 1 pomegranate, remove seeds should yield about 1 cup
- ¼ cup dried rose petals

PREPARATION

- In a large juice pitcher, layer the ingredients with cubes of ice.
  Add fresh filtered water, and keep in fridge before serving.

PREPARATION

- In a large juice pitcher, layer the ingredients with cubes of ice.
- Add fresh filtered water, and keep in fridge before serving.

Blueberry Lychee Mint Water

INGREDIENTS

- 1 cup blueberries
- 1 can of lychee, drained
- 5-10 leaves of fresh mint (depends on leaf size, if smaller use 10 leaves)

PREPARATION

- In a large juice pitcher, layer the ingredients with cubes of ice.

Add fresh filtered water, and keep in fridge before serving.

Blueberry Orange Mint Water

INGREDIENTS

- 1 cup blueberries
- 1 small orange, sliced
- 5-10 leaves of fresh mint (depends on leaf size, if smaller use 10 leaves)

Notes

_____

_____

_____

_____

_____

_____

_____

Raspberry Infused Water

Raspberry Lychee and Rose Water

INGREDIENTS

- 1 cup raspberries
- 1 can lychee, drained
- ½ cup dried rose petals

PREPARATION

- In a large juice pitcher, layer the ingredients with cubes of ice.
- Add fresh filtered water, and keep in fridge before serving.

Raspberry Mint and Lemon Water

INGREDIENTS

- 1 cup raspberry
- ½ lemon, sliced can of lychee, drained
- 5-10 leaves of fresh mint (depends on leaf size, if smaller use 10 leaves)

PREPARATION

- In a large juice pitcher, layer the ingredients with cubes of ice.
  Add fresh filtered water, and keep in fridge before serving.

Notes

_____
_____
_____
_____
_____
_____
_____

Raspberry Blackberry Lavender Water

INGREDIENTS

- 1 cup raspberries
- 1 cup frozen blackberry
- 1 sprig of dried lavender

PREPARATION

- In a large juice pitcher, layer the ingredients with cubes of ice.
- Add fresh filtered water, and keep in fridge before serving.

Raspberry Mint and Lemon Water

INGREDIENTS

- 1 cup raspberry
- 1 pomegranate, remove seeds should yield about 1 cup
- 5-10 leaves of fresh mint (depends on leaf size, if smaller use 10 leaves)

PREPARATION

- In a large juice pitcher, layer the ingredients with cubes of ice.
  Add fresh filtered water, and keep in fridge before serving.

Notes

Citrus Infused Water

Ruby red Grapefruit Rosemary Water

INGREDIENTS

- 1 grapefruit cut into wedges
- 2 sprigs of rosemary

PREPARATION

- In a large juice pitcher, layer the ingredients with cubes of ice.
- Add fresh filtered water, and keep in fridge before serving.

Grapefruit Peach and Cucumber Water

INGREDIENTS

- ½ grapefruit cut into slices
- 1 small peach, peeled and sliced
- 6 cucumber slices

PREPARATION

- In a large juice pitcher, layer the ingredients with cubes of ice.
- Add fresh filtered water, and keep in fridge before serving.

Notes

_____
_____
_____
_____
_____
_____
_____

Orange and Blueberry Rosemary Water

INGREDIENTS

- ½ orange cut into slices
- 1 cup blueberries
- 1-2 sprigs of rosemary

PREPARATION

- In a large juice pitcher, layer the ingredients with cubes of ice.
  Add fresh filtered water, and keep in fridge before serving.

Orange Mint Water

INGREDIENTS

- 1 large orange cut into wedges
- 10 leaves of fresh mint

PREPARATION

- In a large juice pitcher, layer the ingredients with cubes of ice.
- Add fresh filtered water, and keep in fridge before serving.

Citrus Cucumber Water

INGREDIENTS

- ½ orange cut into wedges
- ½ lemon cut into wedges
- ½ lime cut into wedges
- 10 slices of cucumber

PREPARATION

- In a large juice pitcher, layer the ingredients with cubes of ice.
- Add fresh filtered water, and keep in fridge before serving.

Spiced Infused Water

Ginger Cucumber Mint Water

INGREDIENTS

- 6 slices of ginger, washed and peeled
- 10 slices of cucumber
- 8 mint leaves

PREPARATION

- In a large juice pitcher, layer the ingredients with cubes of ice.
- Add fresh filtered water, and keep in fridge before serving.

Lychee Ginger and Cinnamon Water

INGREDIENTS

- 1 can lychee, drained
- 6 slices of ginger, washed and peeled
- 1 stick of cinnamon

PREPARATION

- In a large juice pitcher, layer the ingredients with cubes of ice.
- Add fresh filtered water, and keep in fridge before serving.

Lemon Ginger Raw Honey Water

INGREDIENTS

- 1 cup Raw Honey dissolved in some warm water (do not use boiling water)
- 6 slices of ginger, washed and peeled
- 1 lemon, sliced

PREPARATION

- In a large juice pitcher, layer the ingredients with cubes of ice.
- Add fresh filtered water, and keep in fridge before serving.

The Power of Ginger

Ginger is an excellent ingredient for better digestion, especially after eating oily and fried foods.

Ginger also helps stimulate saliva, and gastric juice production to aid in digestion. It could also help relieve any bloating or gases trapped in your digestive system.

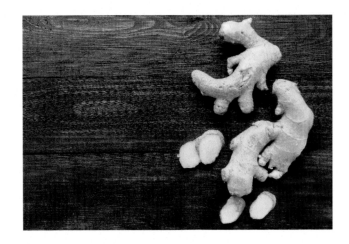

White Pear Ginger and Lychee Basil Water

INGREDIENTS

- 1 large white pear, sliced
- 1 can lychee, drained
- 4 slices of ginger, washed and peeled
- 8 leaves of fresh Basil

PREPARATION

- In a large juice pitcher, layer the ingredients with cubes of ice.
- Add fresh filtered water, and keep in fridge before serving.

Apple White Pear Rosemary Honey

INGREDIENTS

- 1 white pear, sliced
- 1 green apple, sliced
- 2 sprigs of rosemary
- ½ cup Raw Honey dissolved in some warm water (do not use boiling water)

PREPARATION

- In a large juice pitcher, layer the ingredients with cubes of ice.
- Add fresh filtered water, and keep in fridge before serving.

Raw Honey with Chrysanthemum Flower and Ginger Water

INGREDIENTS

- 8 slices of ginger, washed and peeled
- ½ cup Raw Honey dissolved in some warm water (do not use boiling water)
- 1 cup chrysanthemum dried flowers

PREPARATION

- In a large juice pitcher, layer the ingredients with cubes of ice.
- Add fresh filtered water, and keep in fridge before serving.

Honey Chrysanthemum Flower and White Pear Lychee Water

INGREDIENTS

- 1 white pear, sliced
- 1 can lychee, drained
- 1 cup chrysanthemum dried flowers
- ½ cup Raw Honey dissolved in some warm water (do not use boiling water)

PREPARATION

- In a large juice pitcher, layer the ingredients with cubes of ice.
- Add fresh filtered water, and keep in fridge before serving.

Cinnamon Raw Honey with Apple and White Pear Water

INGREDIENTS

- 1 large white pear, sliced
- 1 gala apple, sliced
- 1-2 sticks of cinnamon (depending on how strong you want it)

PREPARATION

- In a large juice pitcher, layer the ingredients with cubes of ice.
- Add fresh filtered water, and keep in fridge before serving.

Chrysanthemum Rose Water with Pomegranate Seeds

INGREDIENTS

- ½ chrysanthemum dried flowers
- ½ cup dried rose petals
- 1 pomegranate, remove seeds should yield about 1 cup

PREPARATION

- In a large juice pitcher, layer the ingredients with cubes of ice.
- Add fresh filtered water, and keep in fridge before serving.

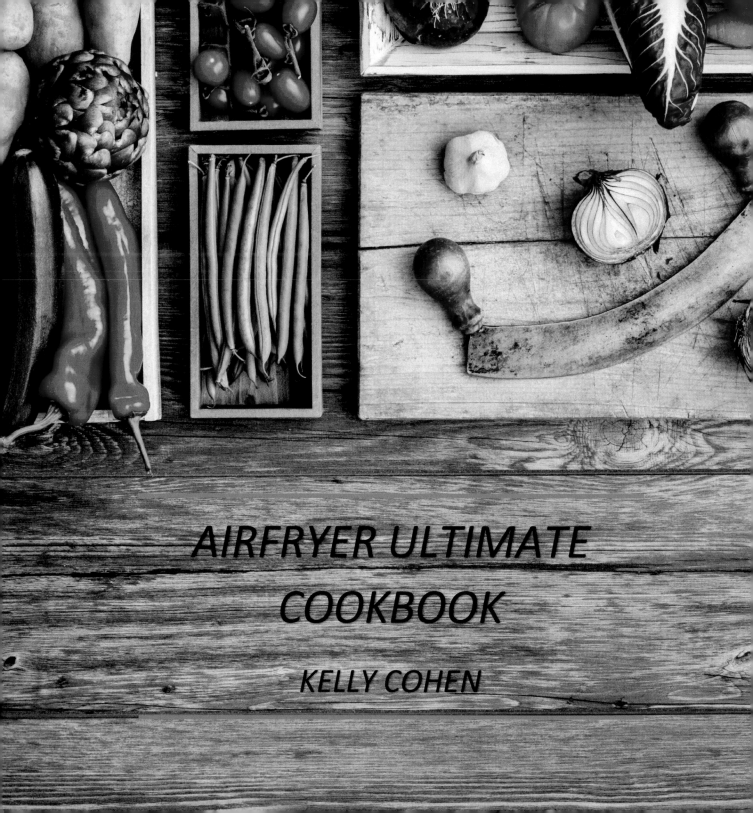

AIRFRYER ULTIMATE

COOKBOOK

KELLY COHEN

Copyright Legal Information

THANK YOU

*We sincerely hope you enjoyed
cooking with us!*

Kelly Cohen

Made in the USA
Middletown, DE
16 December 2017